FAMOUS PEOPLE GREAT EVENTS

Elizabeth I

By Harriet Castor
Illustrated by Peter Kent

W

TTS

This edition 2012

Franklin Watts
338 Euston Road
London NW1 3BH

Franklin Watts Australia
Level 17/207 Kent Street
Sydney NSW 2000

Text first published as *Famous People, Famous Lives:
Elizabeth I* in 1996

© text Harriet Castor 1996, 2012
© illustrations Peter Kent 1997, 2012

The right of Harriet Castor to be identified
as the author of this work has been asserted.

The right of Peter Kent to be identified
as the illustrator of this work has been asserted.

ISBN: 978 1 4451 0867 4

Dewey Decimal Classification Number: 942'.055'092

A CIP catalogue record for this book
is available from the British Library.

Series editor: Sarah Peutrill
Original series editor: Sarah Ridley
Artwork: Peter Kent (line), Rory Walker (colour)
Consultants: David Wray and Dr Anne Millard

Printed in China

Franklin Watts is a division of Hachette Children's Books, an
Hachette UK company.
www.hachette.co.uk

Chapter 1

In 1533, a royal baby was born. The father was Henry VIII, King of England, and the mother was Anne Boleyn, the second of his six wives. They called the baby Elizabeth.

King Henry was disappointed. He and his first wife had already had one daughter, Mary, and now he wanted a son. He thought only boys were any good at ruling countries.

Henry didn't know what a great and famous queen Elizabeth would turn out to be.

Perhaps it is time for a new wife...

Later Henry and his third wife did have a son, called Edward.

Edward and Elizabeth got on well. They both studied hard and wrote each other letters in Latin!

At last. A boy!

When Henry died, Edward became king, even though he was only nine.

But he didn't live long. Sadly he died when he was fifteen.

Chapter 2

Elizabeth's older sister – Mary Tudor –
became queen next.

At this time, people argued a lot about the
right way to worship God. One group were
called Protestants. The other group were
called Catholics.

Kind Edward VI had said everyone should be Protestant. Now Mary I said everyone should be Catholic. No wonder there were lots of arguments!

Mary even made her sister Elizabeth a prisoner in the Tower of London for following the wrong religion. Mary was afraid people might try to push her off the throne and put Elizabeth there instead.

Elizabeth was very brave, even though she was in danger of having her head chopped off.

When Elizabeth was 25, Mary died.
Now, at last, Elizabeth was queen!

The first thing everyone said she
should do was to get married, because
people still thought women weren't good
at ruling countries. They wanted her to
have children, too.

But Elizabeth didn't want to marry. She didn't want a husband telling her what to do.

Chapter 3

Elizabeth was ruler of England, Wales and parts of Ireland.

Scotland had its own queen, Mary Queen of Scots. Mary and Elizabeth never met, but Elizabeth asked other people what Mary looked like. She was jealous in case Mary was more beautiful than her.

Mary is a bit taller than you, Your Majesty.

Aha! That means she is too tall!

Elizabeth loved dancing and music. She wrote some poetry too, and was famous for being an excellent horse-rider.

Tired? Poppycock! We've only just got going!

But Elizabeth wasn't the sort of ruler who just had fun all day and left the governing of the country to others. She worked very hard. Often, she was at work with her ministers before dawn.

And Elizabeth wasn't always easy to work with. Though she was often cheerful and witty, she also had a terrible temper.

She once threw her slipper at one of her ministers, and spat at a courtier she was cross with. Her maids of honour often got slapped.

Rogue! Dolt! Ale-swilling knave!

In public, though, Elizabeth was gracious and kind. She wanted the ordinary people to love her and be loyal to her.

She wanted to impress them, too. So, for public appearances, she always put on her most magnificent clothes.

One of her dresses was decorated with a thousand seed pearls.

Though Elizabeth had expensive clothes, she was still very careful with money. If even the smallest jewel fell off a dress or cloak and was lost, she had it carefully noted down.

Anyone found the diamond yet?

I thought she just wanted us to kneel!

How much did I get for that necklace?

Sometimes she even sold off some of her personal possessions to get a bit of extra cash.

Chapter 4

One of the most expensive things a ruler could do was go to war. So Elizabeth wanted to avoid it.

But in 1588 she didn't have a choice.

The trouble was, Elizabeth was a Protestant, and some Catholic rulers of other countries wanted to push her off the throne and put a Catholic there instead.

Mary Queen of Scots, who was living in England for her own safety, was the centre of several plots to replace Elizabeth with a Catholic ruler.

To protect herself, Elizabeth made Mary a prisoner. But even from prison, Mary continued to be involved in plots.

Eventually, after 19 years, and yet another plot, Elizabeth ordered Mary's head to be chopped off.

But that wasn't the end of the danger.
The Catholic King of Spain, Philip,
wanted to make England a Catholic
country again.

So, in 1588, Philip decided to invade. He
sent a fleet of ships, called the Armada,
to attack England.

Elizabeth's spies told her the Armada was
coming, so she got her own ships ready.

Elizabeth's ships were much smaller than Philip's. But the English sailors had a clever idea.

They loaded some empty ships with gunpowder and set them on fire. Then they pushed them towards the Armada.

Luckily, the wind carried on blowing the 'fire-ships' the right way!

The Spaniards were terrified when they saw the fire-ships. They tried to sail away as fast as possible, but their ships were so big and clumsy that some bumped into each other!

The English ships chased them. Then there was a terrible storm and most of the great Spanish ships sank.

Meanwhile, back on shore, hundreds of soldiers were getting ready to fight the Spaniards if they landed.

Elizabeth went to see them. She told the soldiers that, just because she was a woman, it didn't mean she was scared – she was as brave as any king.

When the news finally came that the Armada was beaten, everyone was very relieved.

Poems were written in celebration, and there was a magnificent procession to St. Paul's Cathedral for a thanksgiving service. Elizabeth rode in a chariot with a golden canopy, pulled by white horses.

Chapter 5

Elizabeth didn't only go out amongst her people when there was a crisis or a special celebration.

In peacetime, to let as many of her subjects as possible see her, Elizabeth went on 'progresses'. She and her courtiers travelled about the country, staying with important people on the way.

Travelling was very slow and difficult. They could only go about five kilometres an hour, and no more than twenty kilometres a day. If the weather was bad it was even slower.

No wonder Elizabeth called the journey from London to Bristol "long and dangerous"!

Having Elizabeth to stay was a great honour. But it was also dreadfully expensive. It wasn't just the food; gifts and special entertainments were expected, too.

One host had a big lake dug in his garden, with man-made islands in it, for a play. And Elizabeth was only staying for three days!

When Elizabeth finally died, aged 69, she had been queen for nearly 45 years. Because she had no children, the crown passed to the son of Mary Queen of Scots: King James VI of Scotland.

He became King of England and
Ireland as James I, and ever since then,
the countries of the 'United Kingdom'
have shared the same monarch.

Further facts

Tudor Toiletries

Elizabeth was famed for being very clean. People were amazed that she had a bath once every three months – whether she needed it or not!

Although Elizabeth's teeth went black in old age, it wasn't because she didn't clean them. She rubbed them with a cloth and used toothpicks too.

The water-closet (WC) was invented by a godson of Elizabeth, John Harington. Elizabeth was so impressed with his idea that she had one installed at her palace at Richmond.

Her courtiers, though, carried on using loos that didn't flush.

They were cleaned out only when the Court moved on to a different palace. Then somebody had a very smelly job!

Fresh Talent

In Elizabeth's reign, there was a new actor and playwright in London called William Shakespeare. Some of his plays – which are some of the most famous plays ever written – were performed before Elizabeth herself.

Some Important Dates in Elizabeth I's Lifetime

1533 Elizabeth is born, the second daughter of Henry VIII.

1536 Elizabeth's mother, Anne Boleyn, is ordered to be executed by her husband, Henry VIII.

1547 Henry VIII dies. Her brother, Edward, becomes king.

1553 Edward VI dies and Elizabeth's older sister, Mary, is crowned queen.

1554 Elizabeth is imprisoned in the Tower of London by Mary I.

1558 Mary I dies and Elizabeth is crowned queen.

1587 After many years of plots and intrigues by Mary Queen of Scots, Elizabeth orders her execution.

1588 Philip of Spain sends a fleet of Spanish ships, called the Armada, to invade England. The English fleet wins and the danger passes.

1603 Elizabeth dies at the age of 69 years old.

Quiz

Can you remember?

1. When was Elizabeth I born?

2. What were Elizabeth's sister and brother called?

3. How old was Elizabeth when she became queen?

4. Why didn't Elizabeth want to get married?

5. Who kept plotting to steal Elizabeth's throne?

6. Which country did England have to go to war against?

7. What did the English sailors do to get rid of the Spanish ships?

8. Which famous playwright lived at this time?

9. How old was Elizabeth when she died?

10. Who ruled after Elizabeth I?

Answers on page 32

Glossary

Armada A fleet of ships.

Catholic Christians who follow the leadership of the Pope in Rome.

Courtier Wealthy and important person who wanted to be close to the Queen and spent time at Court.

Governing Running the country.

Latin The language spoken in ancient Rome and widely used by educated people in Tudor times.

Maid of honour A young unmarried woman from a wealthy background who acted as a helper and companion to the Queen.

Ministers The most powerful people in government.

Protestants Christians with their own set of beliefs. In Tudor England Henry VIII made himself Head of the Church of England, a Protestant Church, and broke away from the Roman Catholic Church, led by the Pope.

Tower of London Where important prisoners were locked up.

Index

Quiz answers

1. 1533
2. Mary and Edward
3. 25
4. Because she didn't want to be told what to do
5. Mary Queen of Scots
6. Spain
7. Set some empty ships on fire and sent them towards the Spanish ships
8. William Shakespeare
9. 69
10. King James VI of Scotland, who became King James I